Wooden Nutmegs

poems

Wooden Nutmegs

poems

by
Russell Rowland

Encircle Publications, LLC
Farmington, Maine USA

Wooden Nutmegs ©2020 Russell Rowland

Paperback ISBN-13: 978-1-64599-073-4
e-Book ISBN-13: 978-1-64599-074-1
Kindle ISBN-13: 978-1-64599-075-8

All rights reserved. No part of this book may be reproduced in any form by any mechanical or electronic means including storage and retrieval systems without express written permission in writing from the publisher. Brief passages may be quoted in review. Rights to individual poems and essays remain with authors.

Editor: Cynthia Brackett-Vincent
Book and book cover design: Eddie Vincent/ENC Graphics Services
Cover Image: Shutterstock.com
Author photo: Colleen Eliason

Sign up for Encircle Publications newsletter and specials
http://eepurl.com/cs8taP

encirclepub.com

Acknowledgements

These "wooden nutmegs" first appeared, often in earlier form, in the following gratefully-acknowledged publications:

Blue Unicorn: "Indian Pipe."

Café Review: "Town Clock."

Camel Talk: "Shaker Meetinghouse."

Chiron Review: "Third Trimester."

Concho River Review: "The Wedding as Opposed to the Marriage"; Under the Tarps."

Connecticut River Review: "A Death on the Budapest-Kecskemet Line."

Except for Love: New England Poets Inspired by Donald Hall (Encircle Publications, 2019): "Dandelions."

Ibbetson Street Press: "Uses of Time."

Illya's Honey: "Cat Cage"; "Swallowtail Visits Violet."

New Zoo Poetry Review: "Scorekeeper."

Northern New England Review: "Falling Leaves."

Off the Coast: "Memorial Exhibit"; "Mud Season"; "What We Saw."

Plainsongs: "Bridal Veil Falls"; "First Day of Fall"; "Last Snow"; "Lumen."

Plainspoke: "Stanton Road"; "Willey Landslide."

Poem: "The Year We Ate Leaves"; "Untended Apple Trees"; "Visiting Her."

Rockford Review: "Two Stables."

Rose and Thorn Journal: "Count It All Joy."

San Pedro Review: "In Season."

Schuylkill Valley Journal: "Secret Annex."

Sky Island Journal: "Carol's Skin Graft."

The Aurorean: "Blue Heron"; "Cow Cave"; "Double-Dammed Pond"; "Early Snow"; "Mouse Tracks on Snow"; "One More River"; "Red Hill"; "Standing Still Near Hart's Pond"; "Thinking of April in January"; "What to Tell a Little Girl about Autumn."

The Cape Rock: "Mosquitoes."

THAT Literary Review: "Testing the Limits."

The Comstock Review: "Countdown"; "Our Little Church."

Tiger's Eye: "The George Cemetery, Holderness."

Toasted Cheese: "Dirt"; "White Gloves."

Wild Goose Poetry Review: "Newspaper Obituary."

Wind in the Timothy Press: "Let the Sun Tell You."

Contents

1.

Wooden Nutmegs 3
Stanton Road 4
Moodus Noises 5
Willey Landslide 6
Shaker Meetinghouse 7
Untended Apple Trees 8
Two Stables 9
Salem Village 10
Brunch on West Rattlesnake 11
Little Boy in Grandpa's Barn 12
Double-Dammed Pond 13
Cow Cave 14
Falling Leaves 15
Our Little Church 16
The George Cemetery, Holderness 17

2.

First Day of Fall 21
Red Hill 22
What to Tell a Little Girl about Autumn 23
Early Snow 24
Mouse Tracks on Snow 25
Thinking of April in January 26
Last Snow 27
Mud Season 28
By a Vernal Pool 29
Bridal Veil Falls 30
In Season 31
Goldfinch in Goldenrod 32
What We Saw 33
Let the Sun Tell You 34

Standing Still Near Hart's Pond 35
Swallowtail Visits Violet 36
Blue Heron 37
One More River 38
Count It All Joy 39
Stealing Apples 40

3.

A Death on the Budapest-Kecskemet Line 43
The Year We Ate Leaves 44
Indian Pipe. 45
Secret Annex 46
White Gloves 47
Under the Tarps 48
Testing the Limits 49
Ring Dike 50
Third Trimester 51
The Wedding as Opposed to the Marriage 52
Bride's Premonition 53
Countdown 54
Letting Go 55
Cat Cage 56
Carol's Skin Graft 57
Visiting Her 58
Newspaper Obituary 59
Memorial Exhibit. 61
Dirt 62
Gone the Sun. 63
Faux Swan 64
Sunday Face 65
Scorekeeper 66
Town Clock 67
Parable 68

4.

Lumen 71
Hairy Woodpecker. 72
Dandelions. 73
Mosquitoes 74
Snow Due Tonight 75
Footprints in Snow. 76
Uses of Time 77
Cleaning House 78
Small-Town Good Friday. 79
Peddler. 80

About the Author 81

1.

*I'm a peddler, I'm a peddler,
I'm a peddler from Connecticut.
I'm a peddler, I'm a peddler,
And don't you want to buy?*

*—"The Connecticut Peddler"
H.W. Dunbar, 1851*

Wooden Nutmegs

Endless dirt roads drift into summer air
as dust, after the footsteps of the traveler.
Heat mirages disappear and reappear.

Where's that rainbow children run to find?
A trick of the retina. Where's the promise
old Noah drank to? Entirely of the mind.

Chimeras—in a sequence of mill towns,
farm villages along the itinerant route—
by him, transmuted into gospel truth.

He is no charlatan. An illusionist,
perhaps. If sleight-of-hand fosters trust,
is he also a peripatetic evangelist?

Hill farmer thinks himself an honest man,
whatever his aggrieved neighbor thinks.
His daughter loves her own pulchritude,

and teaches it to her bedroom mirror.
The farmer's wife? Nutmegs of wood—
as far as appearances go—about as good:

she feels the equal of the neighbor's wife,
believes that sampler about a happy home,
though her pillow stifles cries at night.

Is the next township reachable by dark?
Peddler walks faster with an empty pack,
before any biddy wants her money back.

Stanton Road
1843

Not even with a nod in passing did
his Momma acknowledge the tall stranger,

but he was little—came right out and asked:
"Are you the ghost?" Momma jerked his arm.

The stranger, with an aw-shucks kind of shrug,
said, "Yes, I am." Eyes reddening, brimstone

smoke at his nostrils, he just disappeared
from the outside in: first nondescript clothes,

then the hairy chest and bearded chin,
then bird-cage ribs, pelvis, and death's-head grin,

at last red viscera, his veins, his brains,
leaving only smoke. But Momma, to the boy's

chagrin, tended to grow unsociable
this time each month; today, she practically

pulled the arm from his socket in retreat.
As they fled around the unpaved curve, his feet

grounding at wide intervals, the boy looked back,
and thought, "I'd love to learn to do *that* trick!"

Moodus Noises
circa 1689

By this I surmise they be of the devil,
that they resound arbitrarily before bane
and blessing; whereas if they were of God,
they would always warn of grievous fault.

Yon rascal Raffles Howe insists they be
Lucifer belching. In the tavern one takes
all things lightly, even the sun that smites
men by day, the moon women by night.

A psalm each hour. But how shall the saints
sing the Lord's song in a wilderness
where the earth booms beneath their feet,
to a different meter…and to no Amen?

Oft I behold hunters returning ghastly;
Goody Gooch will not hang out her wash.
Smiles fade, birds fall still. My sermons have
been rudely interrupted, brought to naught.

Thy promised land looks to belong to ogres.
Parts of the forest remain dark at noon;
our settlements, weak and far apart.
Shall we abandon Zion, sail for home?

Willey Landslide
August 28, 1826

There was no time, was there, to describe
the smell of descending earth—
root cellar, crypt, whatever simile
was on the tip of one's tongue—
as the entire geology came down
to swallow all who lived in its shadow.

No time to remark its weight.
That many cubic leagues are heavy as rock,
and some of it is rock. You were caught,
carried along in the postures of your flight:
if an arm stretched out toward safety,
outstretched it stayed.

Eyelids were plastered open, iris to dirt.
Last gasps drew loose mountain into you.
The ponderous planetary weight
collapsed you to the bone, squeezed out
all air; all liquids drained away.
Slowness…silence…nothing.

You were christened Polly, Samuel, Sally,
Elbridge, Martha, Jeremiah, Eliza Ann.
It was a week before they found
the first of you, and three they never found.

Shaker Meetinghouse

Sabbath. Ladderback
furniture hangs on pegs
along the wall, ingeniously
out of broom's way.

Seats of these antique
masterpieces are warm
from a previous, perhaps
recent, possibly invisible
occupant:
        defunct
eldresses sit high, sensible
shoes in our faces.
                Saints
do the dying right, become
extinct, in lady-like rebuke
to our serial generations.

Nurtured four seasons by
the abstinent, wouldn't we,
who nightly grope to couple,
shake, shake out of us
all that is carnal?

What more perfect, in this
of all times the wickedest,
than covenant to not exist?

Untended Apple Trees

Their fruit is riddled, disreputable,
ammunition for pugnacious boys.
The collective, "orchard," yields
to "residential": fruited aisles
represented nowadays by one
gnarled survivor in my yard, one
losing limbs beside your patio.

Logger John's been talking loud
through his lack of teeth about
a chainsaw to cut them as flush
as the returning veteran's stump,
Last Judgment measured by cord.
That motivational fear of fire:
overnight, it seems, they reveal

a fit and comely contrition, that
would commend green novices.
The decrepit go up in blossom,
make night sweet, and all that fly
drunk. No blasphemer can pass
without praising, and there is no
separation of Church and State.

Two Stables

Someone's stabled mare looks out at me
and my backpack, like an elderly widow
who knows passersby steal everything.

Long since, I happened across
another stable, distant in the woods:
grass grew wild through its floorboards,

acorns made hailstones on a corrugated
roof, the manure was dry and odorless.
Work of hands got disestablished, there.

Whatever girl once gazed for hours,
for love, between the rails, her palms
damp from two great inquisitive noses,

watching the proffered apples disappear
in slobber, while she dreamed of a ride
across the firmament with herself astride,

may be rocking on a creaky porch today,
the pulses in her wrinkled temples
like hoof-beats receding into memory.

Salem Village

Pumpkins dot the common, and the wind
is off the sea. My teenager and her friend

step buoyantly on cobblestones Hathorne
and Mather wore smooth at one passage.

Nearby, guiltless Giles Corey croaked,
"More weight," but girls' hearts are light.

Crows that rode gibbets, plucking out
popped eyes, have long since flown away.

Where wretches were innocent, girls stroll
uneven pavement, graceful in denim,

their sentences half-finished in the way
of friends since kindergarten. Souvenirs

accumulate. I pay for sweet licorice,
for everything, as if under some spell.

Note: "Hathorne" was the family
name before Nathaniel added a "w."

Brunch on West Rattlesnake

Let us carry our comestibles
in wicker up the Old Bridle Path,
and except for hiking boots,
dress formal: skirts, jackets, ties.

Our ancestors could do it:
you'll have seen the daguerreotype
of nineteenth century climbers
in cravats, collars, crinoline:
gracious!

We follow them uphill,
to swallow what we packed,
and be swallowed by the view.
We slid wetly after them in birth,

and for sure will follow in orderly
fashion into ash and dust,
drawing our children after us.
Anniversaries, and daily bread.

We're higher than the ravens now,
but lower than the angels. Is it true,
cremation takes two hours? Really.
Then would you kindly pass
the costly mustard with the silly name.

Little Boy in Grandpa's Barn

The old barn listed too far off plumb
to be really safe, but hadn't fallen yet.
Both lock and latch were impotent.

Wasps owned it now, intent unknown,
among beams lurking to bang a head,
tools for which the present had no use.

It was never off-limits to an introvert
who after breakfast vanished outside
among buzzing cicadas and goldenrod,

maybe to reappear by noon. So much
to measure himself against, experience
in the absence of pedantic grownups.

No artificial light, just the aroma of hay
and generations of dehydrated manure;
cobwebs to make a specter out of him.

Yet more than this—he felt there was
a portal someplace off in all the gloom,
a threshold of entrance if not return,

which Grandpa and Grandma crossed,
after they died—she in her lace apron,
he in his overalls. Both lived beyond.

He could turn around and steal away,
back to his parents—or pass that door,
to where the best hot chocolate waited.

Double-Dammed Pond

Beavers dammed it at both ends.
The name took a swamp-Yankee ironist.

First the pasture full of rocks,
then your barn burns down.

The year tomatoes withered on the vine.
The year all cows but Rosie died.

After a boulder breaks your plow,
the roof beam breaks your back.

Bad enough if the mortician calls once.
If he has to call twice, that's hell.

Two stones in a little plot outside:
Abigail, 36. Charity, 12.

In the middle of the pond, a lodge
of many rooms, not made with hands.

Cow Cave

A granite ledge, earth washed from under it
by patient, diligent water, flowing down
through Sandwich Notch. Cow Cave—

so called. A farmer's prodigal cow
spent all winter in the cave, walked out
mooing petulantly that spring—they say.

Yet ruminants must eat. And Lucifer
tested famished Jesus in the wilderness.
We love to hear all stories, true or false.

Mosquitoes rise out of mold, and circle
my ears, homing in, intent on blood.
There are great hungers in these woods,

as everywhere. Folks actually say
chickadees fed that cow. They say
angels came and ministered to the rabbi.

Falling Leaves

This is a time of breakage which initiates
picking up the pieces, with tine and tarp,
among those to whom cleanliness is next
to godliness. And speaking of pieties,

dooryards look much as churchyards might
if their stained-glass windows shattered,
and shards of martyrs landed everywhere.

The Stoning of Stephen is best portrayed
in broken glass; his murder's consequences
in scarlet leaves or fractured maple limbs.

We can also be found on hands and knees,
tending the newest stone in the cemetery,
lest leaves bury it up to or above the name.

We keep dim photographs, olden letters
in boxes—a foliage that yellows, fades—
against next season's loss of memory.

We don't take the damage so personally
as to justify complaining. God will make
everything new. We, who parse infinity
with lengthy stone walls, old cellar holes,
are conscious by now of all we need do:

rake the leaves, and wipe our tears away.

Our Little Church

Straw-filled cushions provoke allergies.
We've a ways to go, to be accessible
to the lame and deaf. Our bell annoys
the neighborhood at wee hours, bulletins
of 1960s vintage flutter from between
the pages of our hymnals as we sing.

Sermons, somniferous. One venerable
soprano screeches like a two-by-four
pulled loose by crowbar. If we attend
regardless, it's because the third person
of the Trinity steals in on occasion,
and fondly musses everybody's hair.

The George Cemetery, Holderness

In birches off Route 113,
where is neither marriage nor giving,
removed from our post-Thanksgiving
insomnia at outlet and mall,
first flakes tuck the Georges in.

The eldest died before Lincoln did,
the youngest never watched television.
The only novelty inside their fence
is one veteran's toy flag,
colorful as a cardinal.

Knowing these alabaster boughs
will bud next spring like growing girls,
while bears grunt out from crevasses
to break their fast, it's easy to be skeptical
of death today.

I must visit you next April—Abigail,
Levi, Charity, 12—when topsoil thaws,
and you kick the covers back.
I can help you make your beds,
find you places in my sleepless world.

2.

Many goods have I in store,
So listen whilst I name them o'er,
So many goods you never saw before.

First Day of Fall

Sunrise first colors the tops of maples, then
gradually condescends to us: below the angels,
soon benighted. Sunset, earlier than yesterday,
leaves us to deal with darkness as best we may.

We have unfinished business: trips not made
to the ice cream shop, now shut; reconciliation
with estranged siblings, which should precede
placing harvest upon the Congregational table.

We who overslept each summer morning rue
these curtailed hours—as if we realize at last
all we might have done. But songbirds piped
and we did not dance; migrated, and we did

not mourn. So in fairness we had our chance.
Now, let us disabuse our children of eternity:
tell them that oil lamps need oil, and it is best
to bring their last tomatoes in before a frost.

Red Hill

Red Hill stands so clear
in October morning air
I feel I could walk there.

Ruddy the hill was not,
from late November on,
but will go russet yet—

like that red fox I turned
from his purposes, along
an uphill trail last year.

So many leaves it takes
to redden a whole hill!—
of similar kind, as well.

(Attend the meeting held
in town in March by us:
far less unanimous.)

A hill next going grey
at the closing pages of
our current calendar

may tempt us into grief,
in the absence of at least
a mustard-seed of faith.

What to Tell a Little Girl about Autumn

Tell her the geese are leaving for a place
where there is never ice on any pond,
and little girls wear shorts all winter long.

Tell her those upright cornstalks in a field
are bridesmaids rehearsing her processional.

Say: while jack-o-lanterns cannot choose
to smile or scowl, a little girl can choose!

Talk about dressing up for Halloween,
to the admiration of indulgent neighbors
and playmates asking that great existential
question: Who are *you* going to be?

Explain what the foliage is poised to do:
turn all the colors in her crayon box,
then spiral down and gather into piles,
to cushion gently life's hard landings.

Tell her of apple bushels, of the farmer
gathering the harvest in, of hands young
and old filling jars to be stored against
the winter months when earth lies fallow.

As birds fly, leaves fall, tell her of spring,
when much of what we love only to lose
is given back. Of course, not everything.

Early Snow

October in New Hampshire: many leaves
still in oak trees, defying a rake's outreach.
Watching flurries from my window seat,

I think of old friends, how they show up
sometimes: unexpected, out of the past,
out of yearbooks, without phoning first—

and one is grateful, more or less, even as
the trip to the coast is mentally cancelled.
One has anticipated seeing these friends

at the resurrection of the godly, just not
today—and they are not always as one
remembers them, if one remembers them.

Unpredicted snow squalls do their ballet,
frosting late foliage—the yellows, reds—
dusting our lawns with a patina of age,

though it is not winter, barely Halloween.
The fat jack-o'-lantern must blink a flake
from his socket, and the corn stalks shake.

Mouse Tracks on Snow

Deer, moose, and I left holes, not prints—
but you, O mousy, did not weigh enough
to break through. You walked upon snow,
your traces like the touch of fingertips.

Between the double trail, a line as straight
as a pencil's: you drew that with your tail,
bringing up the rear. Doesn't it get cold,
poor naked string, or freeze inflexible?

Are there predators about, who need a lot
of you and yours, to make a decent meal?
No wonder your eyes are as beady bright
as those of a frightened child. One blink,

and nasty old owl has you: I would see
your trail come to an end at a disturbance
in the snow, imagine you hanging limp
from the talons, your first and final flight.

This world is all diamonds from the sun
today, in our not unlimited succession
of winters—the pair of us making tracks
toward some lost Eden. Spring, perhaps?

Thinking of April in January

As thumb nudges the thermostat, and frost
curlicues plate glass, my lethargy becomes
a remembering of old lovers, former wives.

I dwell on grandiose eruptions of crocuses,
meadowlarks out-warbling angel choruses,
picnics in paddocks free of ants and ticks;

boyfriend beside girlfriend, hand in hand
under cirrocumulus, confident of a future
shadowed by neither death nor divorce.

But was it so? Have I forgotten anything:
mud-time that never ends, a killing frost,
the daisy-petal's oracle, she loves me not?

I'll abide this month we are living now,
stalled as it is, a still life in monochrome;
and this apparition between the dresser

and bed, silhouette shrouded in flannel.
Yet in my reverie spring peepers chime,
day breaks early, and its hours are warm.

Last Snow

Of its attraction we have had enough;
of its descent from pristine into slush,
more than enough. This is the time
to feel finished with what we know,
without asking, will come back at us:

to have so satisfied all bodily desire
that a body will never desire again—
until tomorrow; cancer in remission,
though terminal; our last word upon
the subject circling round to haunt.

We stare out the window, eager for
novelty of season; in the mirror, for
change of face; across the kitchen
table for variety of companionship.
Sleepers awaken to return to sleep.

Enough? There are lines that read
that the changeable will be wrapped
in changeless cerement—a promise
they trust in the little white church
in the village, where time is different.

Mud Season

It is that recurrent chapter in our lives
when assets liquidate. The water table
rises out of the ground like a vampire.

Dirt roads are mud-baths for vehicles.
We scrape boots off in the doorway,
not to be barred by our Better Halves.

Poor mud-stained Girl Scouts peddle
cookies after school. Compassionate,
we order more than we will ever eat.

Pastor pronounces us modern saints.
He knows better, but earns his bread
helping us forget our name is Mud.

The Town posts weight-limits on all
back roads. Reserve no moving van:
this month you'll neither come nor go.

Suspended animation: if sextons dug
at the cemetery, graves would fill up
with water. The dead too must wait.

By a Vernal Pool

Every subsidence in the April forest
fills with tea—the tea-bags, saturated
leaves of oak and beech—soon to be
drained by the summer's rabid thirst.

An unseen frog stammers something
amorous. I empathize: I've stuttered
in courtship, with indifferent results.
How be fruitful, then, and multiply?

Gelatinous clouds of eggs transmute
to tadpoles, overlooked by overlords
of the world's distress. Occasionally
a limb is missing from an amphibian.

Fragile, fractured, life insists on itself
in pool and burrow. A few offspring
survive, seeming less than their sires,
less competition for a pool's princess.

The mirror-image is blue, though less
than yesterday. I examine it for birds
no longer heard, spring-times birthed
in the innocence of childhood—well,

for Eden. As old fools will. Instead,
there in a windless sky is the contrail
of one of the empire's winged beasts:
a long white etching, clean to the kill.

Bridal Veil Falls

The strait-channeled millrace unfurls
over these ledges, like a frilly scarf
in June's breeze. Thus teased out
in attenuation, it receives a name.

We have struck the poetaster's pose
to christen it after our rite—because
it is always about us, because human
is human measure of everything—

as if a cascade overspreads the allure
of a bride's face, misting blemishes
and ambivalence, when she's escorted
to her oceanic destination, matrimony.

A groom parts the protective curtain,
finds flesh of his own flesh: in effect
mirroring his own face. Adam likes
what he sees in seeing what he's like.

Now, God does put asunder. Knives
of ice split rock. A river separates us
from the promised land. Continents
drift apart, as if their marriage failed.

To any vista does a dowry accrue?
Yet we hear in the treble of the falls
a variation on the Song of Songs:
"No falling water quenches love."

In Season

Out front, on schedule, the Tiger Lilies all
show off, like ostentatious neighbors.

In the nearby Ossipees, Wood Lilies
take their bows of simultaneous debut—
along mountain trails through sunny dells.

Nature, it seems, still makes everything
beautiful in season, despite climate change
and so many oblivious heads busily texting.

We had our time, my dear and I, but now
it is our season for assignations after dark,
when imagination's fantasy flourishes
and thrives, like orange lilies here and there.

We droop—as do petals of yard and woods,
their moment past. This is preordained:
not even the most insouciant escape it.

We walk into the little graveyard, fenced
and full, names fading from worn granite,
long grass rippling in the wind like waves,
a few plastic flowers forever in season.

Goldfinch in Goldenrod

Goldenrod bows to a wind that blows anywhere
it will, and fixes the trajectory for flighty finch—
which, wherever it alights, shall find sustenance.

Quickened spark seeks tinder of complimentary
color, that will rekindle incandescence in accord
with a Word that gilded and pronounced it good.

I seek such gold forever—but cataracts develop
on lenses that have avariciously looked for gain.
The flower appears colorless, the feather grey,

grass withers, songbirds wing away. That bow
of many colors in the sky goes black and white.
The forecaster will make no guarantees tonight.

Midas, Midas, chance gave you a golden touch.
But grapes turned into nuggets when you ate.
Your harem became statues. You learned late.

What We Saw

Wasn't it Labor Day,
was it Whiteface or the other—

We crossed paths at the summit, you
with your mother, son, and daughter;
both kids wanting lunch, missing their dad;
your still-married sister. The dog
nosed everywhere: scrub pine, my crotch.

We saw a hawk balance on its high wire
between heaven and intervale,
boat wakes etch white scratches
in that blue window, Winnipesaukee.
We mistook Kearsarge for Cardigan.

I could tell you took the children everywhere.
You saw how your son stared up at me.
I knew the wind's direction from your hair.
Each saw the other's ringless ring finger.

Let the Sun Tell You

Let the sun tell you
where the cobwebs are.
Follow it around the house
all day. Surprise them.
They think you can't see.

Let the sun tell you
where dust is laid like snow.
Lift up the doily, and Aha,
a dust doily remains;
you've invented an art form.

Let the sun tell you
when a year gets old.
It cuts back on its hours.
Homeopathic pills on legs,
spiders no longer cower.

Let the sun tell you
the best way out of here.
It sets without struggle, has
no unfinished business,
rises again another place.

Standing Still Near Hart's Pond

Stasis arouses the curiosity
of timid things, feathered and furred:

chipmunks approach my halted boots,
chickadees hop closer, twig by twig.

I extend a finger on an extended arm—
then wait. Someday, if my unworthiness

does not exceed that of the centurion
who asked healing only from afar,

one of those grey-white bobbins will alight,
and make a story everyone hears twice.

Swallowtail Visits Violet

Commerce of ephemerals. Petals
easily support like weightlessness.
Touch subsists in its moment—as
manna in wilderness. No covenants
upon granite. A brief zephyr kiss.

Black-barred yellow wings fan gently:
lover's languor. Consent is neither
given nor withheld—as it used to be
with us, when we were primeval, and
did not even know we were naked.

Sip. This is my nectar, secreted
for you. Today is all. Because
there is no memory, there can be
no yesterday. Because there are no
cares, there need be no tomorrow.

Fly. Clear the treetops. Weave
a flight-path through white pine,
red oak. God said to pollinate,
multiply. Let it be to us, His
servants, according to His word.

These part, to be forgot, forget;
never in this world to meet again.
But there will be another butterfly,
visiting another violet. Eternity?
One small blossom to balance on.

Blue Heron

Its origami narrowness
is suited to its essentials. We,
obese, should be so blessed.

Thrashing in the scissors of a beak,
dinner splashes silver everywhere.
God holds the food-chain tight.

Concentration
is a Great Blue apparition
motionless in its reflection
in the mirror of Shannon Pond.
We should stay so focused,
who multitask—

a patience which ensues
from willing just one thing.

Slow steps to better angling
make not a ripple that
might alert a fingerling:
more prudence than have we,
where to set two feet.

Outside the pecking order, I
am distraction in morning mist.
Wings flap like lazy laundry
into the woods. May we

be as forbearing, with
our annoyances.

I buy time for the fish.

One More River

Kayakers paddle, duck-like, along
banks of the tannin-colored Contoocook,

disappear round a bend. Wakes fade
off the glossy page. My parallel

course jogs down this riverside trail:
the water is scenery, not my medium.

Yet we reach the same place, a bridge
for traffic whose pilgrimage crosses

one Jordan more. They must live on
the far side, or there wouldn't be bridges.

They must all be feeling far from home,
because there are so many rivers.

Count It All Joy

As I reach this age of inexpensive delight,
gratitude's teardrops blur the watercolor—
wildflowers to bless another highland hike.

We haven't met before, but their imagery
persists, back home. "Drooping bell-like
flowers, backward-pointing tubular spurs":

thus an Audubon volume introduces me
to Wild Columbine: now and for a while
a delicate, unassuming, newfound friend.

Years younger, I resented the immortality
not given us, to match every blossom to
its name, each songbird to a song and call.

I would have chafed also at the thought
of such fragility so near the trail; of what
a more oblivious pair of boots might do.

Full of the present, I didn't dream a day
was appointed when I would be as glad
of endings as of beginnings; dark as light.

All flesh is grass. The flower on the hill
fades. But a hummingbird has reached
the nectar just in time, so count it all joy.

Stealing Apples

The peddler in passing pilfered them
only from the ground, most bruised,
some brown—still, not his ground,
no one to forgive him his trespasses
except himself, and a dog to outrun.

Not divine, this one. Yet the width
and breadth of Eden opened to him:
he helped himself, as Adam would,
in a garden without boundaries, no
stone walls parceling God's creation.

Appropriation will not make anyone
a god, but something actually worse:
arbiter of right and wrong. Suddenly
good has its opposite, Eden borders
Nod. Snakes appear, ripe apples rot.

One must eat. The peddler is aware
his sin is not original. See, sparrows
are pecking the windfalls too, and he
is worth many sparrows—the Bible
ballasting his backpack tells him so.

3.

Here are pins,
Papers and needles and pins,
Tracts upon popular sins,
Any of which I will sell you.

A Death on the Budapest-Kecskemet Line

"We were delayed perhaps ninety minutes…"

Passengers began to socialize; you found
this incongruent with the tragedy ahead
and beneath—once a Hungarian student
with some English informed us the train
stopped after it hit and dragged someone.

We jerked forward finally. Both later
agreed that we felt a sympathetic shiver
where we sat, as our car went rattling
over ties from which the *disjecta membra*
had just been removed, by latex gloves,

a forensic team, as policemen watched.
Derangement—suicide—alcohol—
we never heard. Waters, deep and to us
impenetrable, of the Magyar language
and culture swallowed up the incident,

in a land where life manages to go on
in spite of even worse things. Someone
somewhere is surely crying, someone is
always crying somewhere. Government
does what it does best—nothing—and

then the priest comes, with one old lady
in a babushka, who is as ugly as a saint:
God let her live to be a hundred, so
those too distrait for orthodox prayer
at least have a bosom to cry upon.

The Year We Ate Leaves

There are times, and ways of telling time.
The clerics, bearded with vehemence, insisted
we tear up all calendars: Western, Gregorian.

So you were born the Year of the Dust Storm.
Your witty uncle named the Year We Exported
More Sorghum Than We Kept. And thus,

"the fullness of time." A moment that is not
hallowed is a moment that never happened—
as our divines, in their fanaticism, insist.

I have visited the camps, air shimmering
above them with radiant heat of thousands
of bodies, the moan of voices all at once

praying in despair, daily haphazard burials
of bagged burdens, large and little ones.
Fat cargo jets parachuted much generosity

from fast-food nations, landing haphazardly;
somehow little of it reached the square miles
of tents. Next, our crops failed, and cattle

became bone-cages, and you died. It might
have been 1988, possibly as late as 1992.
To us, it is just The Year We Ate Leaves.

Indian Pipe

Corpse plant, ghost plant—renouncing sunlight,
minding its business deep in the dark understory
where secrets proliferate and memories flicker,

like foxfire. Such pipes are little of our affair,
their peace forever beyond our understanding—
we, whose souls sight along the barrel of a gun.

How pale is the pipe, from many puffs. It needs
no chlorophyll. No incense fragrant to a divinity
whose minions are foreigners in their own world.

I wish the pipe would pass to me—from whom
the cup of bitters would not. I desire, above all,
mercy for the penitent detained inside my skull:

caged bird. I bring confession as burnt-offering
to the sparrow's raided nest and the empty cradle.
I seek absolution from ancestral apparitions, half-

transparent, who walk from the woodland carpet
to the surface of the pond, then across it, making
neither wave nor sound, impervious now to harm.

Pass the pipe. It is the hour for me to reconcile
with witnesses to what I did: their village torched,
their screaming children silenced by black smoke.

Secret Annex

Bookcase gets slid aside from hidden door,
with no browsing of motley titles shelved:
Deborah, Queen Esther, Ruth Expatriate.

Evidence of recent habitation: silverware
in the sink, unfolded laundry, two pencils
on a table, and what turns out to be a diary.

They will perhaps be coming home soon?—
the family—from shopping, from the opera,
from that party at Papa's office downtown.

Intruders thumb a couple pages, smudge
the cursive of a girl who despite everything
believes that people are really good at heart.

They miss the framed photograph: she lacks
a woman's poise; knock-kneed, but the eyes
hold eternity, and the picture will remember.

Back outside, they loiter beneath a crockery-
colored Amsterdam sky, without horizons
and only stoned crows to scribble across it.

Uniforms lounge at the street-corner, shift
over, work done. We were not our work,
they will inform a tribunal, after the War.

White Gloves

When the bullet hit (she never heard
the shot) she fell among the leaves
of autumn, to die as they had died,

right in her own backyard: thirty feet
from home, eighty from the woods—
says the police report. It was the talk

of central Maine. You may be aware
of that moisture in the eye when folk
feel sympathetic? It did not appear.

Recent arrivals from New Jersey, he
retired from Princeton, she his wife;
no hunters, not a gun between them.

The hunter, local man, given benefit
of the doubt—lack of judgment firing
near a residence less harshly judged

than her wearing of white gloves
outside, in season: a kindergartener
would know better. Her widower

returned to New Jersey. No charges
were brought against the hunter, who
must be elderly today, if still alive—

outdoor days past, rifle hung above
the fireplace; his bag, from forty-plus
seasons: no deer, only one housewife.

Under the Tarps

Heavy tarpaulins conceal both cars
destroyed in the head-on, each askew
on the closed highway. Occupants
are still inside, there is no urgency

to remove them. Pending arrival of
the medical examiner and notification
of next of kin, two tarps protect
the privacy of the accidentally dead.

Underneath industrial-grade shrouds,
those who left home washed, dressed,
breakfasted Somebodies, are suddenly
Everybody—collective and generic,

drained of originality as of blood,
deprived of idiosyncrasy as of breath.
So many acceptable, productive ways
of living, but only one of being dead.

Tarps, however soiled, are not without
reverence: palls, if you will. Personnel,
assembled upon the pavement with
little more to do, can do that much—

professional courtesy. They've seen
this or worse before; will soon return
to (they assume) less-transitory lives—
eat nutritious suppers, bed the wives.

Testing the Limits

Trombone-voiced counselors regiment
their troops for the descent. One boy,
discovering a hideout among the ledges,
drops out of sight. Tan arms, bare legs,

towhead, do not answer to their muster.
What if he stays. How many miles until
they notice—one sheep short of a flock.
He observes his stasis with detachment.

Flickering in memory, the candle flame
attracts a slow finger again. The needle
from Mother's sewing box slides easily
underneath his skin: such is experience.

Last August he stood on railroad tracks
that converged to a shimmer, watching
the brilliant eye grow brighter, bigger—
only to see how long he could face it,

how much a life in North Newington
Junction was worth to him, what sort
of option death was, whether parents
should be listened to in such matters.

Oh, he did break and run. The freight
roared past him unheeding. But today,
on the summit, he hears young voices
fade, imagines his face on the posters.

Ring Dike

We take our ease with walking sticks
on old carriage roads that together knit
this nine-mile circumference.

The summit blew its top,
then collapsed into its own cauldron—
apocalyptic display. Not yesterday.

What remains of a mountain
is no longer tumultuous, but in repose:
grazing sanctuary for the moose.

Earth outlives the traumas, as
some people do. Recall that article
we couldn't stand to finish:

injured toddler, jailed stepfather,
teddy-bear crying in its broken crib.
O Lamb of God, who bears it all…

We come upon a wood-lily glade,
another Eden. Survivors could reclaim
pillaged childhoods here, and bloom.

Here seedtime reaches harvest,
all safely gathered in. Another child,
beaten by her mother, died—

we would like to find
her, done with dying, in the glen,
chasing monarch butterflies.

Third Trimester

She brings to Senior English, as to Show
and Tell, the unborn baby's ultrasound,
her son afloat and almost viable,
conceived as she was, eighteen years ago.
Just one reaction is equivocal:
"Have it printed in the yearbook, Mel."

College will wait, her mother hopefully
calm down enough to let a baby sleep.
The dad, for whom her sweaty flesh
was as much to handle as a landed fish,
works a cash register somewhere else.
He doesn't answer calls, text-messages.

The Wedding as Opposed to the Marriage

Today, it's easy:
knowing left hand from right,
the way it was explained
at the rehearsal last night.

Tomorrow, harder—that right hand
not always sure what the left intends.

For now, there are promises,
repeated after the minister, phrase
by phrase: in sickness and in health,
in plenty and in want. (Also when sin
is an open secret, all over town.)

Sara and Edward, beautiful
and handsome as expenditure allows,
no one except perhaps the creditor
expects you to be seeing past today.

Love is different than you think.
Pull up the shade on a drizzly morning
while egg sticks to the pan,
and take a closer look at her or him.

In thirty years, after the second opinion,
and the person beside you here
seems not to be listening,
then you will understand.

At best, you'll "make it work."
Today, your photographer has
arranged you perfectly, as only he
and the mortician can.

Bride's Premonition

The death that parts, according to God's Word,
will be yours, dear Love. I do not wish it; such
are the odds: see how the pews fill with widows.

A husband used to sit with each of them, until
he traded bed for box, and she faced the hour
of reckoning: to the thrift shop his good suits,

Christmas cards signed by one, his tenor voice
erased from the telephone answering machine,
living features imprisoned in a photo frame.

If refusal of wedlock could prolong your life,
I would leave you at the altar in an instant—
but you are eligible: another would finish this.

Instead, I promise in the sight of God that I
will so cherish our seasons as to find my cup
half filled—like theirs, who still cheer us on.

Be spared, at least, the sentence pronounced
upon me today: a leaden spirit, ebbing tide
of desire, autumn's red sunset watched alone.

My finger trembles at the icy touch of a ring.
I swell with your rationed breaths. Against
my heart beats your heart—counting down.

Countdown

In five seconds his phone will ring.
This is about those five seconds.

He is savoring the fruity aftertaste
and buzz of a red wine purchased
an hour ago at Rite Aid, of all places.

His shoes are off, his belt unbuckled.
The workday and its duties are done.

Fifteen miles away a nail-polished
fingertip is tapping his number.
We know, now he must know.

In one more swallow, he will know.
For a long time to come, he will
remember these last five seconds

of ignorance of what lies ahead;
this daily, bottoms-up, feet-up belief
in the complacent goodness of life
and of others—which is ignorance,

which is bliss, which is ephemeral.
This is about those five seconds.
His are upon him, yours are coming.

Letting Go

Old oaks are reluctantly relinquishing
hoarded leaves onto an upstart snow.
Somewhere beneath corrugated bark,
trees might ponder that they brought
nothing into this world, and will take
nothing out—as the chainsaws buzz,
and the woodstoves send up incense.

After Max died, you could see a lot
of sky. He fell in the bathroom late
one night: a coronary cut him down
like an axe. Loggers of sorts arrived
in an upholstered metal-grey palfrey.
Max rode stiffly to the pyre, his burn
reddening the heavens, and our eyes.

Jane still lingers, in the family forest,
releasing her leaves of grieving, since
the season calls them down that she
submitted to at the altar: Until death
parts us, which of course was never
going to happen, during the vernal
April and febrile August of marriage.

The oaks, most of them, will endure.
Jane? No remarriage in the forecast.
But when joy returns—twig by twig,
leaf by leaf—through grandchildren,
sunrises, sunsets, Christmas caroling,
she may join such arboreal remnants
in the seedtime, and grow more rings.

Cat Cage

Today Marion's friend Emily brings
Mr. Whisk in his cat cage for a visit,
to this home where living is Assisted,
dying discouraged—but permitted.

Marion's loneliness really gets across
to the younger woman: how all hope
can curl up and quit in an easy chair.
You could die of tender loving care.

It is hard for the youthful to identify
with old age. But Emily understands:
no room to turn around; a look at life
as through wire—a kind of kitty cage.

Marion loves cats. You notice a row
of photos on the bureau: all the cats
she has outlived, just as she survived
a daughter, a husband, and two sons.

See, she emerges from her lethargy,
while Mr. Whisk is relieved to find
it isn't the vet's! Cat gives new life
to the old woman—one of his nine.

Carol's Skin Graft

She will come home from surgery
knowing how it feels to be
a patchwork quilt, with pilferage
from here to cover there:

mortality's Ponzi-scheme.
Scars, age spots, varicosities. We
are not youths, luring paramours
to our seamless epidermises—

no, we just pray to reach
tomorrow in what is left of us;
our priest the dermatologist,
sacrificial knife in his latex fist.

Carol feels cheekbone and chin:
the skull within
maintaining an embarrassed grin
at the thought of being out of skin.

Nurses, temporarily beautiful,
look in, move on. Carol is
their mirror, their crystal ball:
they want her well—and gone.

Visiting Her

We won't stay long. She tires,

watching, watching the hours:
children who scamper past
on their way to distant beds.

Don't feel you must prate
in the pauses. Eternity
seems shorter to her than to you.

Don't be caught pitying.
Shadows that grow with afternoon
look to her like forty angels
bringing her pair of wings.

Don't hold her hand today unless
you've held it every other day.

If the meds convince her she
is Mother Teresa, act leprous;
if Lesbia, Catullus.

If at all, hug gently.
Her bones are ribbon candy.

Newspaper Obituary

...died Saturday, surrounded by...

You had me surrounded? Oh my god:
no opening in the circle, no escape
back into health. For the death of me,
no such privacy as even dogs enjoy,
creeping off into the underbrush to die.
Lachrymose circumference! Crocodiles!

...after a brave battle with...

I did not battle, and I was not brave.
I submitted, in fear and trembling, to
all the incomprehensible, polysyllabic
diagnoses, the poisonings, irradiations.
Clammy, I lay awake all night, as Asrael
took shape above me, irrevocable...

...predeceased by...

Fine word. The bastard beat me to it.
He left me without important papers,
without any chance to forgive and be
forgiven—left me bodily, having left
long ago in spirit. His legacy includes
a dent in the cushions. Oh, and shoes.

In lieu of flowers...

Yes, spare me the florist's grandiosities—
give to The Society for the Prevention of
Upstaging the Corpse. Flowers deceived
me all my days into expecting Paradise

beyond the death certificate. Or in lieu
of everything, just let me rot in peace.

Memorial Exhibit

Her framed photography lines the walls.
The Africa series, including that giraffe
with a bird clinging to its lengthy neck.
The India series, proud scowling faces.
The Amish series, men and their sons:
straw hats, suspenders, really bad teeth.

In the room, upon a table, photographs
of the photographer, such as callers see
at a funeral home. Her figure thickens
with time; her eyes wise up, innocence
to experience—while horizons widen,
from the domestic to the international.

There's her school portrait, maybe age
ten, "SHM" for Sacred Heart of Mary
embroidered on a jumper. Her smile
asks no questions of us, God, anyone.
Gabriel hasn't appeared, to prophesy:
When you are fifty-seven, in the fall,

cancer will be diagnosed. By spring,
it will have sampled every vital organ
but your sacred heart. Now go, fulfill
your calling while you can. We see it
through her lenses. She did her best
to be the handmaid. We are witnesses.

Dirt

After weeks of stoicism and tuneless whistling,
Barney finally broke down over Adeline's box
at the edge of six cubic feet of topsoil, severed
worms, about to separate him from his pretty girl

of fifty-two years. We looked away, embarrassed,
looked instead at the dirt: restful emotionless stuff,
with its potent sexual fecundity: almost any crop
can grow—except another Adeline won't come up.

The blindness of topsoil, against our open eyes,
the deafness of it, working its way into our ears,
the dumbness of it, impacted in our throats,
the impartiality of it, burying sinner next to saint—

we well understood the blackness inside Barney's
one suit, as he in turn began to concede to the dirt,
to trust it with Adeline; to walk away, let her melt
into dirt forever, as into the arms of another man.

Gone the Sun

Bugler, straight as a flagpole, wafts
consolatory opening notes of "Taps"
into memorial air and receptive ears,
on the greenest lawn in town. His war
won, our neighborhood veteran's
Day is done.

Alive, one more unremarkable man.
Dying has elevated him in the esteem
of his widow, who changed the sheets;
adult children raised absentmindedly,
grandkids living far away from home.
For these, here gathered, *Gone the sun.*

Pastor notices, mortician confirms,
aside—the perfection of the rendering,
without cracked or mangled notes,
while the legato bugler doesn't seem,
between the phrases, even to breathe:
From the lake, the hills, the sky.

In fact, that bugle is playing itself,
via computer chip, without assist
from the regalia—striped, creased—
that handles it. Technology consoles,
more sure than fallible lungs and lips.
Fading light. Dims the sight.

Virtuosity a sham, bereavement real;
between, Job's controversies lie:
Shall he live again, once a man die?
Mourners depart, reassured for now
by melody unfurling like the flag.
All is well, safely rest, God is nigh.

Faux Swan

Meredith Bay has become Swan Lake,
but defecating geese are not abashed
by what neither trumpets nor attacks,
merely floats at anchor day after day—

any more than their flock was taken in
by coyote sculptures that never barked
or chased. Gagging town employees
must still follow up with shovels, pails.

I on the other hand was *quite* deceived;
told Facebook friends to come and see.
Always the fool: mistaking heirlooms,
drapes, and samplers on a parlor wall

for a happy childhood home, when all
along, words snapped bone like sticks.
Parental parts were played by lunatics.
So I grew this alabaster curving neck,

rode picturesquely on the River Styx,
receiving compliments and coverage.
An inner hollowness kept me afloat.
Passersby were never ornithologists.

Geese still waddled along the bank,
gabbling, squabbling—unimpressed
by artifice. I was unreal, they sensed.
And any place geese gathered, stank.

Sunday Face

White gloves, anachronistic Sabbath hat,
her rebukes to the casual anything-goes
informality of a congregation's clothes,
these days. The tight marmoreal smile,

her churchgoer's face. It looked as if
the Spirit pulled corners of her mouth
apart from behind, each Sunday at ten,
and thus they froze, till the last Amen.

Lips did not need to speak, to identify
her as a pillar, one to whom the homily
must appeal for approval; whose tithe
could be conferred or withheld at will.

The smile rose superior to anger, pain,
unmentionable matters, including how
a stepson baited her on infrequent calls,
or what a husband left her in the trust.

It easily survived that scandalous urge:
tear off the hat, right there in church,
beat a loveless breast, and stand alone
in front of everyone, in need of prayer.

An embalmer preserved it faithfully
for her rose-lit wake. At the cemetery,
Pastor saw it right through the wood,
and knew the eulogy better be good.

Scorekeeper

When you're small and do the chores,
and it's not your turn, you get a point.

When you're old and a cheerful candid doctor
informs you the tumor's there to stay,
and you go home, wash dishes, fold the clothes,
let the cat in and out, you get a point for that.

You get one point for each soft answer spoken
through clenched teeth to a hormonal teenager.

You get a point not just for allowing your hubby
his old *Playboy* Magazines, but for your straight
face if he swears he reads them for the articles.

You get a point by not saying something stupid
like, "It was coming apart anyway,"
when you drop the Christmas ornament
your wife's grandmother made as a little girl.

If a neighbor's husband dies,
and you bring a casserole even though
they built the spite fence, that's one point.

For not keeping track of your points,
you get a point. For sharing a few of yours
with some pointless person, you get a point.

Town Clock

When the wind is right, I hear the strike
of our downtown steeple clock.

Though inconsistent as to the date
His own Son rose from death,
God knows what time it is.

While sub-Saharan babies starve,
we Congregationalists, according to
our polity, are arguing the cost
of an automated winder for the clock.

Christ be our judge: he was hungry,
and we did not feed him—nor recall
to set that clock ahead in spring,

back in fall—disciples forever either
early or late to church, and some
forever singing his praise off-key.

I vote we let the clock run down,
like time itself. When all stands still,
expansive galaxies will have reached
their apogee; begin the long collapse

down to a dot of matter infinitely,
inescapably dense. No giving
in marriage then, or taking in eulogy,
no orthodoxy and thus no heresy;

no past or present or future tense.

Parable

A pillar of the Congregational Church
raised hands to heaven, thanking God
he was not like other men—"Not like
that peddler there, defrauding wives
with wooden nutmegs, skipping town,
a widow's last farthing in his clutches.

"I fast twice weekly, and give a tenth
of all I have to church and charity."

The peddler in question stood apart,
not lifting even his eyes to heaven
while he prayed, but beat his chest:

"I have swindled the least of these,
Your children, with my facile fakery.
God, have mercy on a sinner: me."

I tell you the peddler, not the pillar,
pleased the attentive heart of God.

He who thus himself commended
was abased; he who himself abased,
commended. Yet pillar persevered
in tithing, peddler in bamboozling,

and God in loving both of them.

4.

Here are knives,
Ribbons and silks for your wives,
Whistles and jew's-harps and fifes,
On which your sons will play sweetly.

Lumen

While the age of many,
in obituaries black and white,

I have yet to release the firefly
I cupped in my hands, a child
of ten in Connecticut at night,
in a moist meadow flickering
with thousands of its kind—

my palms not burned
or even warmed, no more
than Moses by a burning bush;
than my skin by the full moon
of my tenth July: moonlight

without heat, as in the face
of a beloved who doesn't love
you back. That spark I held
intensified, till I could see
fingers' veins and bones.

All ten fingerprints,
circuits of charged wire.
I wondered if everything
I came in contact with
would catch contagious fire,

yet be unconsumed. A boy
began to understand how cool
to the touch is poetry.

Hairy Woodpecker

We picture him nesting at the dark
of a long day: headache, sore neck
from hours of hammering, beak

worn down to nothing—read
into feathers human frailties.
Measure of all things, us.

In age's twilight, I prefer
to be instructed by the bird—
song and call, avian mating ritual,

distinctive markings, diet, range;
how to distinguish male, female;
Hairy, Downy—all the while

keeping out of sight and trill,
no distraction from the will
to live, the living for a meal,

survival long enough to breed.
Witnesses need not impose,
observer be observed.

Bird hops, trunk to limb,
giving bugs the needle; takes
whatever the season gives—

in his world of lows, of highs,
its weathers, and its winds…
and one bush with eyes.

Dandelions

As far as eye can see—
a buttery Milky Way overspreads
acres of May's green firmament:
weeds by profusion transfigured
to a new Eden, equally transient.

The very same eye narrowed
at the Samaritans, at the poor
we always have with us—a squint
that let in neither color nor beauty;
that delayed no errand at the sight.

The mowers perhaps are waiting
to throw their rotary blades
into noisy high gear, and leave
a harvest of severed yellow heads
for vintners, for brewers of tea.

Spared the grim reaper's scythes,
those button-blondes will whiten
like other once-young brevities,
until breezes sweep them away
from stem and root and memory.

The eye itself starts to go opaque:
no yellow, little hope, less light,
until the surgery. Healed, it waits
for withering winds to moderate,
sells all it has, and buys the field.

Mosquitoes

A mile into these humid woods,
I swat. A speck of fluff goes down
to the leaf mold, quickly replaced
in line: same appetite, same whine.

I understand the passion to live,
to be outlived. I feel it. How can
it burn so fiercely in things so small?

That professor and his wife,
of hearsay: their pact was suicide—
the passion to die together, prepense;
family acquiescent, told in advance;

the children all raised to maturity,
every chapter read twice, the chronic
turning acute, the acute terminal.

I understand this too. A day I took
as boy's due, feckless boy in shorts,
sunburn peeling, became precious
as it ebbed, yet will grow wearisome

when body can no longer bear it.
That night, the mourners will hover
and bend, keening like mosquitoes.

The book borrowed long ago
must finally be returned.

Snow Due Tonight

The air is dense with imminence,
for in the clouds an army gathers,
greater than the Heavenly Host
that taught us In Excelsis Gloria.

Something is happening up above
that never did before, a new thing
morning forecasts underestimated,
in deference to the shoppers' rush.

Heaven is astir, prepared to come
in swaddling to earth. We inquire,
Whose birth? Possibly our own—
an astonishment, not so welcome,

messing with the made-up mind.
Orange convoys wink yellow eyes;
try to plow it all under, yet cannot
obstruct the traumatic obstetric.

Knowing familiar things will pass,
and secrets of each heart be read,
we nervously await evening's first
soft touch on the upturned face.

An advent: what will come of it?
Meteorologists are quiet. Joseph,
what was that dream that made
you cry aloud last night, in bed?

Footprints in Snow

...And the end of all our exploring
Will be to arrive where we started
And know the place for the first time.

   —Eliot, "Little Gidding"

Now is the season to bushwhack
through stilled woodlands in quest
of your Avalon or Zion; maybe find
an abandoned graveyard, maybe remains
of some old mill that ground the corn

or sawed the logs; or discover wreckage
of a plane-crash many years ago
that made headlines since recycled;
or else some ridge and gully never seen
before by optics such as yours;

even to play at being what some day
you'll be for good—since getting lost
is a revocable counterfeit of death:
friends and family worrying identically
into their phones, same empty bed—

knowing your footprints on the tabula
rasa of winter will lead you home again,
because, however far you wander, home
is where you're going, like Odysseus.
He found suitors courting; what will you?

Probably you will see them seeing,
with different eyes, a different you.

Uses of Time

Good neighbor Dan came over
with his obstreperous snow blower
while I was still in the shower
this morning. Dan saved me an hour
of shovel work; thus I could phone
to see if my two ladies were at home:
sweetheart, and daughter.

"Teach us to number our days,
that we may get a heart of wisdom"—

a world behind every mirror,
entire landscapes that await
inside an ornamental Easter egg,
with its peephole at one end,
daughter's and sweetheart's faces
secure within;

the thoughts of a little snowman
inside that globe one shakes
to start a blizzard in miniature:
he discovers the curve
of the universe upon itself.

In the time it takes flurries to settle,
he'll have loved, and lived a little.

Cleaning House

I walked through Ossipee Glen this afternoon.
A silver birch in giving up the ghost had filled
the Whitten cellar hole with splinters of itself.

Unfortunate, the Whitten family away and all,
from their non-continuing city—and a chaos
of sticks to greet them when the trumpet calls.

My own windows needed washing, the carpet
vacuuming, et cetera. But, we do thus: assist
a neighbor, to the neglect of private interests.

Mosquitoes for witnesses, I carried branches
from the Whitten's hole, until the foundation
stones were groomed for their homecoming.

So—lift up your heads, O downfallen lintels,
that children since aged and gone may return
with glad chatter, and parents smile on them

once more who rest in the burial plot uphill;
night skies be richer with stars than our sky
in its poverty; that Bossy moo like long ago,

and scripture be read at night in the absence
of glowing screens; loves last, vows uphold;
one candle shine again in memory's window.

Small-Town Good Friday

Between noon and three o'clock,
school bus processionals
red-light the two-way traffic.
Forgive them: texting motorists
who don't know what they do.

Blue strobes beyond the square
stop a car that departed town
a little too speedily. Officer quips:
"Not the best way to Paradise!"

Life in our maternity wing goes on.
A son beholds his mother there;
a mother beholds her son.

Calling hours at the funeral home.
"Why have you forsaken me,"
widow asks embalming specimen,
displayed in a rose-lit parlor.

Sports play on two wide screens
at the tavern. Waitress knows
when her customers are thirsty.

A door slams between Jill and Jack
in their modular home. Both tried
really hard. It is finished.

Into the hands of surrounding hills
we commend our spirits.

Peddler

From the bar-lines of summer twilight
the pennywhistle ditty fades, erased

by high humidity. No ovenbird or vireo
reprises it, nor waking memory retains.

The pilgrim's last call is History, a town
of cellar holes, where the turnpike ends.

Citizens need no merchandise: time has
not established the labor of their hands.

There was marriage, giving in marriage,
but all the children died or moved away:

jobs in Lawrence, Lowell, the Midwest.
Second growth took back the pasturage.

The gristmill decreases to rot and rust,
an old church harbors the Holy Ghost.

Traveler finds home here, earthen plot
cut to fit him, once the pack comes off.

Modest hope matches a peddler's claims:
death, like the nutmeg, not what it seems.

About the Author

"Yankee peddler" Russell Rowland grew up in Connecticut, and now peddles his poetic wooden nutmegs in New Hampshire. An ordained minister in the United Church of Christ, he served churches in both states. In retirement, he is a trail volunteer for the Lakes Region Conservation Trust, a judge of local Poetry Out Loud competitions, and an infatuated father and grandfather.

Rowland's poetry has appeared in over a hundred small journals, two chapbooks, a previous full-length collection, *We're All Home Now*, from Beech River Books, and the Encircle Publications anthology, *Except for Love: New England Poets Inspired by Donald Hall*. He has received seven Pushcart Prize nominations.

www.ingramcontent.com/pod-product-compliance
Lightning Source LLC
Chambersburg PA
CBHW060408080526
44583CB00012B/503